Resembling A Moth

John Queor

Edited by Flor Ana Mireles

1st Edition | 01
Paperback ISBN: 979-8-9869891-1-2

First Published February 2023

For inquiries and bulk orders, please email:
indieearthpublishinghouse@gmail.com

Printed in the United States

1 2 3 4 5 6 7 8 9

Indie Earth Publishing Inc.
| Miami, FL |

INDIE EARTH
PUBLISHING

Resembling A Moth

John Queor

Table of Contents

"We may enter and leave this world alone
But while you trot on this soil
You are not alone"

Excerpt from the poem
Fruit of the Forest

Suicide & Crisis Lifeline:
988

Substance Abuse & Mental Health Services Administration:
1-800-662-4357

Graphite

I've had a speck of graphite
In my hand since I was seven
I think it may be sentient
The brain behind the poetry
That steadily flows out of me
At three thirty in the morning
While the rest of the city
Is comfortably dreaming
I'm describing my sadness
I'm a poet by injection
The tiniest small dot
Is the biggest part of me

John Queor

My Darkness Can Never Be All Gone

My darkness can never be all gone
Those gallows are pertinent to my art
I break the bone to set it once more
I escape in the morning undeformed
Dissolving in the acid of my dreams
Diluted promises and vivid seams
You never know when
You'll never see me again
There's a silver lining to my suffering
I time travel and assess the patterns
Resting amongst ten thousand pages
The anthology to finding my freedom
My darkness can never be all gone
There's a silver lining to my suffering

GRATIAM

I feel this static gratitude
That seems to always rise
Even solidified in my blue
Viscous like craft glue
Stuck in my solar plexus
Clogging the natural flow
Inhibiting my chi to glow
And my eyes to moisten

I feel this static gratitude
Vibrating at my crown
Reminding me kindly
That it's okay to be down
Most of the Earth is blue
The wind gets angry too
We are all part of a cycle
Rising and then falling

Like temperatures
Like breaths
Like stars

House Warming

Sometimes I can't believe
The peace I've found here
Surrounded by soft orange
Dead flowers encircling me
Smoke slowly crawling
Resting and dissipating
On the popcorn ceiling
I don't think I ever thought
I would have this feeling
Of almost weightlessness
I won't lie and say it's perfect
There are still the battle drums
Echoing from the red walls
Of a slightly used heart
There are days that
I set up camp in bed
With no desire to escape
The heavy grip of my sheets
But most of my days now
Are in reach of peace

Lion's Roar

Cancer season is coming to a close
I've never been more ready to fall
Deeper into the summer season
I'll drink in the sun and warmth
The aggressive energy of Leo
Replacing the complacent trickles
Of tear trails and internal wars

There are impressions on my palms
From holding on for such a long time
To things that needed to be elsewhere
I am notorious for repeating this offense
I always chose to dissolve in acid vats
To keep the energy comfortable

Cancer season is coming to a close
I've never felt the need to sob lonesome
In my car because of the temperature
Or to sell all of my things and move to Maine
Or choose myself over anything else
But here I am and here we are
Preparing for that lion's roar

Cocoon

The rapids have simmered to ripples
Soft movements upon the surface
And I can sit at the edge of the stream
Look myself in the eyes as I drink
Let the cool spring water dribble down
To nourish my dreams freshly sprouting
To blossom under the waxing moon
As I clearly state my affirmations

I am right where I'm supposed to be
My choices have lead me right here
To cup my hands together and hydrate
To watch my aspirations flourish

The rapids have simmered to ripples
As I lounge on thick lush wheatgrass
Where I feast on all of the fruit that
Grew on trees I thought would perish
Because I didn't know what I was doing
Because I didn't quite trust myself
Because for a while I was just a kid
Who couldn't tear through the cocoon

It'll Be The Fifth Time

I navigate alone
Through the quicksand
I slip
Into a brand new surface
A pane of glass
Holds me here
I slip
Through cold water
Sparkling
Falling
From my crown
To the porcelain floor
I slip
Beneath the sheets
To fixate on anything
Everything
I slip
Through your fingers
Like hourglass sand
Building up in mounds

Soon
I'll be someone new again
It'll be the fifth time

What Spring Does To Snow

Even my shadow is finding the light
Specks of iridescent diamond glimmer
Like when morning sun hits the snow
I've given myself permission to glow
And permission to let things go
In hopes that I may continue to grow

There's a chaos hungry to consume
I feel it even now here in my room
It whispers to my lowest self
That I don't have all that much to lose
But that's no longer my avenue
I've risen and can see the sky

Even my shadow is finding the light
Blushing from soft sunlit brushing
Vibrating like bees gently buzzing
I've given myself permission to glow
And the strength to let things go
Sort of like what spring does to snow

The Fool

Etch an eye between my brows
So that I may see further into
Deeper within the whirling vortex
Of abyss cooing to me softly

Gentle requests that I not
Drop my pebble down the well
A splash will never echo back
And I'll fall until time is decimated

Not that I'm entirely dedicated
To keeping things linear
But the universe is strange
And I'm a good listener

Lemongrass Tea

It must be alright
To dwell on chaos
For a little while
At least

The candle is lit
On my gratitude shrine
Swaying aggressively

It can not always be
Sunflowers and honey
That is not balance
That is just a dream

Chameleon

Chameleon
Who could you be now
Someone I resonate with
Or the pieces of me that I hate
Is there sunshine in your smile
Or has everything gone gray
I think I'm still the same
In each of the good ways
Less eggshell and more beige

Chameleon
Who could you be now
Have you found your colors
Drinking in the pastel dawn
Is there sunshine in your smile
Everything changes after a while
And we're still splashing in the cosmic sea

My Fear Is Just Fibers On The Mattress

There's a silhouette in the window
It escapes with the help of cool wind
Racing so quickly into the shadows
Before the sun decides to ascend
Splashing gold fragments in beams
That caress my face like the breeze
And I know I'm safe once more
From the apparition dwelling lonesome
Waiting for the night to fall
For the world to become so quiet
That its whispers become shrieks
Small slivers of crystal clear memories
Penetrating into the meat
All the times I couldn't be kind
To the child crying in my core
And for a while I would listen
Melt into a puddle of black goo
Just eyes gazing out horrified
From the fibers of the mattress
But now I keep my structure
My bones do not grow cold
The shrieks are whispers once more
My fear is just a fiber on the mattress

Afternoon

Maybe I'll spend more time in the sunlight
There's only so much to see in the dark
Signs in the pale clouds calmly drifting
With diffused warm rays like spotlights
I could venture out and smell the roses
In fields where the green doesn't get cut
Unmanicured meadows to rest within
Like a prolapsed womb to nurture me
Blue and red berries staining my lips
I drink from the cool brook trickling
Release the grip on my manifestations
Trust Apollo to kindly guide me back
To the comfort of a waning crescent
Where in days to come will be
A new moon sat somewhere above
Watching me as I fall in love

With myself

Terrence Tells Me

Terrence tells me to
Feel my feels
So I'm feeling them
They're so unclear
Transitioning endlessly
Taking fast turns
Sedimentary to boiling
I feel self-soothed
Then abandoned
In a millisecond
And I breathe
So deeply
Reminiscing on
Golden mornings
Midnights alone
Solo confabulations
Reading furiously
So darkly strewn
On the loveseat
Convincing myself
I am something loveable
I am deserving
I am growing
I am doing
Fine

Valentine

When love pours down
I open my umbrella
I crawl inside of myself
I search for shelter

I don't want to catch a cold
From standing there soaking
Waiting for the praise to sour
To circle back to my mistakes

When love pours down
I wrap myself in cellophane
I'll absolutely asphyxiate
One way or another

Drought

My love was once an ocean
Incredibly vast and endless
But the sun was terribly cruel
And drank me nearly dry
Only leaving droplets behind
To exist as tears in my eyes

I'm lost in sprawling desert
That once I did navigate
Using stars as my focal point
His heart was my due north

My love was once an ocean
But all things crash and burn
Evaporation leaving only crystals
To glisten in the eager sun
Reminiscent on being young
And flowing like virgin chi

Stew

City lights burn before me
From the window of my dark room
Where I try to trick myself to sleep
Plead with my mind to go mute
But alas begins the slideshow
A merry go round of bittersweet
An eclectic slew of memories
Painting a soft smile on my face
But very quickly tearing it away
To let the pot boil over on the stove
To let the pot fall from my hands
To crash against the tile floor
Emptying the contents everywhere
Like a wound that couldn't close
And I sit amongst the mess
Trying so hard to self-soothe
Without deciding to drown again

Dark Dreams

There is still a war in the center
Although no longer candy-coated
It's not healthy to be too sweet
But hints of honey shine through
Because I can't always be blue
Pastel flashes in the dead of night
Colliding with storm clouds rolling
Staying calm but never knowing
How deep my mind will descend
Seldomly floating in moon beams
But close enough to the surface
Submerged but not in total darkness
Waiting for the blush of morning
To further slither into sleep
Where I dream of the apocalypse
Or polishing off bottles of liquor
Or the ocean angrily crashing
But these are no longer omens
Just demons I invite in for tea
When I wake up illuminated

A Memory, A Feeling, An End

It's hard to find a focal point
Everything is spinning so fast
I think time is different for me
It feels like none has elapsed
But I lose something every day

A memory, a feeling, a friend

I can take a breath and travel
Ten years back in just a blink
Where I remember his love
And all the heartache after
Falling back five years prior

A memory, a feeling, a friend

My gratitude is absolutely endless
But I fidget at the thought of growing
Much older than I already am
All the loss hidden a few blocks up
That will collect like car coins

A memory, a feeling, an end

Siberia

This exotic cruise was just a ruse
And now here we are turning blue
Black fingertips reaching to brush
The icicles from beneath my eyes
And I hope you know I did try
But I don't think I'm made for love
The gusting rush of silver sting
Has followed me all of my days
And I did enjoy to bask in your rays
But I can't live on warm sandy beaches
I descend back into myself like degrees
And I take the icy stairs down further
In depths too dark to consult the mirror
And it's getting so cold as I slip into sleep
With hopes that you'll bundle up tight
And find your way out of Siberia

John Queor

Wick And Wax

The end of wick and wax
Swirl of smoke dissipating
Unseen due to the dark
Now enveloping the room

Two bodies entwined
One is sleeping
One is reaching
His arm will collapse

Decorated in bruises
Almost all of them unseen
Almost all of them internal
Unfixed by ice or sleep

The end of wick and wax
A soul is slowly separating
From underneath the sheets
From the grasp of its mate

Petrified

My butterflies are petrified
Placed in shadow boxes
Painted and polished pristine
They shimmer and they gleam
Perched on plastic wood
Above paper shredded grass

It used to be terribly sweet
The taste of mutual adoration
Now I am sodium chloride
A teardrop in the sea

My butterflies are petrified
They don't visit your shrine
Or meander into your pockets
They sit stale in their shadow box
Waiting for someone new to bid
And be equally disappointed

John Queor

Swept

Nothing will be how I imagined
I have to repaint all of my dreams
Power wash the smoke-stained walls
Tear the polaroids from the mirror
Find new ways to fill the free time
That once was spent here but not
Swirling in the whirlpool of chaos
That I almost allowed to swallow
That I almost hoped would swallow
That makes me sick to think about
I've spent so much time uncomfortable
I keep my feelings in the junk drawer
I shove everything in and slam it shut
I just want constant even pressure
I can feel all of the dips and rises
The pain that trickles in the bloodlines
The hundred foot mound of dirt
That has been growing under the carpet
That makes me sick to think about
That could swallow me if fixated on
If I hadn't tried to fix myself

Vantablack

It sleeps in the pit of me
The words I won't even speak
Through the secrecy of poetry
Some things I keep to myself
Vantablack
Ouroboros
Only I can destroy myself
Feed on the darkness
Replace it with light
Achromatic
White
It sleeps in the pit of me
Waiting to escape
Like a swarm of stars
With colorful wings
To land on your nose
And eat your sickness

The World

I asked the cards why I felt so low
The world appeared to me
I felt a sense of understanding
Reminiscent on all my ended cycles
Never taking much time to grieve
Everything is dissolving around me
Wisps of smoke disperse until clear
And I can see what I'm doing
And I can look at myself longer
And I can let this sadness flow
I'm closer to the alchemy of my soul
My aura is turning into gold
I asked the cards why I felt so low
The world appeared to me
And I know that I have to
Push forward

Between

There's such beauty in *being*
Observing it all so quietly
Crickets communicating
Empires slowly crumbling
And I am in the middle
Cradled thoughtfully
Betwixt heaven and hell
Between happy and sad
Standing at a crossroads
Sometimes almost numb
Other times on fire
Mostly dry tear ducts
But the ocean inside
It roars and crashes
It reaches for the stars
It drags down ships
It floats so peacefully
Observing it all so quietly
Betwixt heaven and hell

Subzero

Do my eyes sparkle from bewilderment
Or is it just residual sadness seeping
Between the lines where I reside
Waiting for an embrace that came too late
There were times I wanted to be numb
I dreamed of the day the feelings faded
The red syrup coursing through me
Alchemized into gelatinous black goo
That expanded like wings around me
Protecting me from the wind of your words
Chilled like ice water after a breath mint
Years spent gnawed on by the frost
But when exposed enough to the cold
The ability to feel begins to subside
I was blessed to be caressed by subzero
My dreams were coming to fruition
When I was sober I didn't feel a thing
Until the soft warmth of bourbon
Let all of my ghosts back in
After winter came the spring
And summer was spent in the sun
I have still yet to fully thaw
Although my edges have softened

I Hope You Know

Chaos can be home
We were formed from it
I'm sure you know
Bacterial mutation
Gasses and star shards
It's all quite simple
Not too complex
It's okay right now
For it to be a mess
We're all just falling
Through space
Through cupped fingers
Through mattresses
Into strange dreams
Forced conversations
Hasty departures
Lonesome prayers
I hope you know
It's okay right now
To just exist

God Knows

The first time I ever drank
I knew it would be a problem for me
My mind is always running marathons
Fixated on memories and possibilities
Situations that couldn't ever happen
Outcomes that could only happen in dreams
After a few drinks my mind loosened
Everything was immediately less extreme
I knew the slope would be very slippery
I'd never felt as free as when the spins came
I tumbled so freely into the darkness
I was disconnected from everything
Tucked into a peaceful warmth
That would try and consume me
But too much of a good thing
Isn't a good thing
We had a good run
At least I
Think we had fun

The Way I Used To When I Smoked

Is it an art form to slow it all down
Photographing moments passing
Inhale the deepest breaths
Releasing them cool and slow
The way I used to when I smoked
Taking time to see the right-now
Focused on minute details occuring
Like seeing a stranger genuinely smile
Or a sweet cat lounging in a sun spot
Driving fast while the sun is setting
Loud music wrapping gently around
Enveloped in beauty and sound
Like a turning point in a movie
And everything feels so cinematic
Small scenes cut and blended
To when you can look at yourself
While still truly being yourself
Hundreds of different perspectives
Like staring intensely directly
In the reflection of a disco ball

Medicinal

I take myself back
To that beautiful afternoon
Laying in the soft grass
Watching the blades sway
And the clouds roll
Laughing over nothing
Listening to *No Quarter*
For the very first time
Captivated by the noise
And the deep breaths
That crept and left
In such perfect harmony
I miss the mayor of weedsville
And the tent in our backyard
I miss Shopping Town
The scene kids smoking
Passing around their bowls
Then meeting in the food court
To ruin my vegetarian streak
On General Tso's chicken
Garlic pineapple pizza
Crawling down the stairs
Laying on a hill at sunset
Lounging atop the jungle gym
My memory is decorated
So vividly in rising clouds
Of aromatic flora
And days I'd return to
In a heartbeat

Sunshine Paradise

I'll find you in the sunshine paradise
Nestled amongst the other diamonds
Appreciating the soft breeze kisses
The warm licks of pale orange beams
Casting your iridescence everywhere
Casting your iridescence onto me
I'll drink in the endless colors glowing
I'll sit and appreciate your shrine
I'll do this for all who I have lost
Before I collapse into mine
Where I will finally let it all go
Where together we will all shine
Where there is no sorrow
Where there is no time

Peace Tea

Building up my tolerance for silence
No sound most usually is the loudest
But lately I've been listening
And saving my two cents

Something to jingle in my pockets
As I pace through the apartment
Reminiscing on all the noise I made
Pointless fights and aggressive bass

Finally I'm turning a new leaf
Plucking and drying that new leaf
Steeping and sipping on that leaf
To reflect and give myself peace

Belladonna

This isn't exactly refreshing
But changes must be made
The petals hit the floor
There's only stems and thorns
Soon will come the ghostly chill
Of autumn's full belly sigh
Rustling the golden leaves
Before they too descend
As blankets tucking in the grass
Those trees will survive
And so will I
To emerge on the other side
Waiting for spring to arrive
Maybe then I'll blossom
You can watch me bloom
A poisonous purple star
Who listened and learned
From the ghastly gusts
Who called me Belladonna

Lady Spider

Lady spider wrap me in your silk
Let me rest peacefully elevated
When the time comes to feast
Only take the bad stuff and leave
So I may climb down the harp stings
See the colors in full vibrancy
As I once did as a child
What feels like yesterday
What feels like centuries ago
Everything's so hot and cold
How much I have learned
How little I know
Lady spider wrap me in your silk
When the time comes to feast
Take only the bad stuff and leave
There's so much left here to do
There's so much left here to see

Held

As I rested in your arms
I was reminded
That I'll return to
The other side
With grand stories to
Whisper again into
The vast womb
Where I'll be cradled
And nourished
Suckling on stars
As my scars shrink

As I rested in your arms
I was reminded
That I can return to
These small moments
With true gratitude
Whispering thank you
Into the vastness
Of wild adoration
Cosmic connection
To be birthed
And loved again

Margie

A huge piece of me still lives
Years back in the North Country
I can still taste the fall air
Smoking a cigarette on Main St.
Crunching on the leaves
I'd make my way to the park
Home of the Lifesaver and
The golden eagle arch
Nineteen seems so far away
I was trying to get it all done
Get the experiences over with
I regret taking advantage of time
Something I thought I had more of
With someone who loved me
When I didn't think I had any
I thought that I was so sly
Sneaking off to smoke
Like I did when
I was living with my grandpa
I had crept out one afternoon
To go for a "walk"
To discover a
Crystal ashtray
Placed on the wicker table
Nothing got past her
I'll never not miss her

Much Like Matter

Where does the wasted love go
Has it been tossed in a landfill
Covered in soiled clothing and bad food
Could one be out there dumpster diving
Drawn strongly to another man's trash
Is any of this worth anything
What of the love that I've discarded
Is it just returned to the sender
As if they've written down the wrong address
Is it feasted on by junk yard animals
I don't think I feel it anymore
I once radiated the essence
Maybe it's in another dimension
I would think much like matter
It can't just be destroyed

238,900

I mourn those still amongst me
But I refuse to stunt my growth
It's hard to keep myself on track
The demons whisper and dance
My visualizations sometimes blur
They seem billions of miles away
It could just be an optical illusion
It may just be a dark intrusion
Something else to slip away from me
I mourn those still amongst me
I often go back to visit the memories
But I refuse to watch myself regress
Two hundred and thirty-eight thousand
Nine hundred miles
Until I'm glowing on the moon
Stay there for a year or two before
Leaving this galaxy for a new one
There's more than enough room
When you get out of your own way
If you get out of your own way

Bartender

Immersed and distant
Caressed by harsh blue
Neon lights in the window
Where I gaze out with wonder
If I could even achieve better
Better yet deserve better
Or if I've burrowed right
Into the place I'm meant to be
With my soul dripping down
Into the drip buckets
Where I'm seemingly shaken
And inside something is stirred
And the ice is cold but sour
And the rim is all salt when it's
Meant to be sugar
And I think to myself
Isn't this neat
But it's not
It's poison and rocks

John Queor

Sodium

My salt hardened in the sun
My ducts are always dry
No matter the storm severe
Or dreams to be elsewhere
With dew collecting in me
As hope starts to ascend
And my stem slowly bends
Following the moving light
Until I'm fully horizontal
Spilling my very small sea
To be taken in by the green
Perhaps returned much later
By generous precipitation
When I yearn for golden light
Instead of the tedious gloom
Alone in my dark room
Contemplating the years
Behind and quickly approaching

Rehomed

Grass is the greenest somewhere else
I guarantee it's over the pond in Iceland
Sometimes I contemplate packing a bag
But I fear it's always the same everywhere
I know the grass isn't the greenest in Arizona
Cars that double as flattops in the summer
But that heat might beat the monotony
I can live with a front lawn made of gravel
This merry go round makes me dizzy
I think it was much worse when I drank
I feel a little less connected lately
Like Pluto drifting off to a new galaxy
I never imagined being so comfortable
Could somehow make me so uncomfortable
I want to piss off to Greenland
Carve my poetry into the ice
Freeze the continuity of this monotony
Breathe air that isn't stale
Gaze into eyes I've never known
I want to be rehomed

John Queor

Sand Glass

The hands whirl so quickly
I always scoffed when I was told
I would feel how I feel right now
Fingers tangled in my hair
Leaving little strands of silver
Small cracks beneath my eyes
That will widen and sink
I'm not too low about it
But conscious of the sand
Already coating the base
Piling upon itself and spilling
There's so much pressure
To get the ducks in a row
To check off all of the boxes
Leave a little something behind
To be remembered by
For as long as possible
There's so much to do
Before the last of it slips
And the glass goes stagnant
But I won't be around for that
So I guess it's none of my business

Man On The Moon

Man on the moon
Mind if I join you
To fish for constellations
Extract their secrets
Release them back
To the sea of stars

Man on the moon
Mind if I rest here
In the contours of
This quiet crater
To drift comfortably
Into Pisces waters

Man on the moon
I won't stay too long
I just need to get away
Escape all of the gravity
And the ennui
It's all so beige and mundane

I dream in deep purples and blues

A New Sun

The world feels too small
It gets a little hard to breathe
When I think about it deeply
There's so much nostalgia
Swirling all around me
And I know very clearly
This isn't my first time here
But it could be my last
And from that thought
I feel extremely relieved
My soul will be a seed
Planted in new soil
Rotating a new sun
Learning new lessons
Affected by different
Constellations
And I'll breathe
I'll feel free
For at least a couple
Lifetimes

Gravity

Ripples upon the reflection
Show kindness to the disturbance
It has to endure the depths
While clarity disperses
Sunrise is only hours away
I can feel the warmth already
I know it doesn't stay gold
I know it can get colder
Breath leaves in wispy strands
Rising hastily for miles
In time to wrap around the moon
I'll be wrapped in soft silver
Progressing while remaining
Absorbing all these changes
Everything is subtle at first
Yet I can't quite remember
Ever going up the slope

Winter Reminds Me

I could get lost in this blank slate
Mounds of cold white for miles
It doesn't quite feel that long ago
Watching crystals cover the tracks
Laughs escaping as vapor fog
It was all falling apart so fast
But also somehow coming together
Etching hearts in virgin snowfall
With red noses and cracked lips
And dreams to also escape in spring
It all just feels like yesterday
But I'm plucking silver strands
And can no longer count on hands
The years passed since then
But I'm becoming the version
Of the person I wanted to be
When I was keeping it together
The best I could with what I had

Covered In Dust

There are parts of me still healing
Despite believing that they wouldn't
I am grateful for how far I've come
Content with where I was
Never waiting or wishing for
A more elevated outcome
Forever blessed and imperfect
Like the most golden apple
With a bruise on its backside
Photographing perfectly until
Examined three hundred and sixty
If you like what you see
I encourage you to watch
I am a butterfly covered in dust
Very much *resembling a moth*
A wild storm is brewing
The winds will fiercely blow
To freshen up my wings
And bring back my glow

John Queor

Tolerance

Back in my blackout era
Dark cloth covered my eyes
My routines were muscle memory
Each curve and bend was expected
Each of my mistakes were backed up
By a monologue and an apology
An excuse dressed in Sunday best
Lacking the power to change
To climb back into the driver seat
Resist the urge to binge all night
On moderately priced gas station beer
And the leftover liquor I couldn't finish
From just two nights prior
Because so long as I didn't imbibe
Multiple nights in a row
I didn't have a problem
I just had a tolerance

John Queor

Give It To Myself

I've got so much love to give
And I don't even give it to myself
I keep it way up on a shelf
It just sits there by itself
What a waste of wealth
Dull and covered in dust
Years of broken trust
By most of all myself
I've got so much love to give
And I don't even give it to myself
I need to clean that shelf
Declutter the memories
Set my love free
And spoil myself

Resembling A Moth

Butterfly Kisses

When the time comes you'll find me
Shimmering in the afternoon ultraviolet
Blue eyes searching the lush fields
As the breeze bunches up my long hair
Wafting soothing aromas of lavender
To dance around you like a butterfly
You'll extend a hand for me to land
To taste the crystalized salt of your skin
And flutter off into the blurred horizon
To meditate on the authenticity of you
Of your eyes and gentle sincerity
Dreaming to land once more upon you
The second time I know that I'll know
I have no desire to be taken away
Preserved in a subconscious shadow box
To be gawked at and forcibly cherished
I just want to be able to close my eyes
My skin pressed sweetly against yours
To wake and be taken by the wind
To choose to return to your soft skin
Without it being an expectation

Three Of Swords

In the shadows you watch me
I smell the tobacco permeate the room
The scent of a passing thunderstorm
There's no lightning without friction
My sheets smell like lavender flowers
You could lie between them for hours
Rest between each of our quarrels
I'd kiss the scars on your shoulders
Bless the three wounds on your back
Engulf you in a cloud of my own
Sip upon your not-so-subtle brooding
Are we alive if we aren't hurting
I'll let you slither away one hour
Prior to Apollo climbing back
From his journey to Australia
I'll be right here when you need me
I'll nurse your wounds again
As I forget my own

Romanticizing

Pastel dreams
Rushed sunset
He's blushing
Softly speaking
No restraint
Graceful fall
Slight obsession
Busy thinking
Autumn stroll
First kiss
Ocean dipping
Desecrated sheets
Love letters
Wedding band
Peace lily
Couple cats
Morning touches
Coffee brewing
Glass breaking
Slamming brakes
Coming down
Dreamy cloud
Shaken awake
Dreary reality
I'm always
Romanticizing

Heliotrope

This emptiness was important
I got here quicker than anticipated
There's so much air around me
A vastness that's unfolding
Like a red carpet
What goes up must come down
So I can't help but imagine that
What goes out must come in
I'm sending my doves to scout
To drop blossoms of heliotrope
In hopes that you can find me
Relaxed on overgrown grass
With my eyes swimming in the sky
My hands drinking in the earth
The breeze ushering you towards me
There's too much air between us

Carcinogen

I wanted to fade into your gray sky
Exit your lips in a swirl of smoke
Some special Camel blend or
Seneca if you're still struggling
Although forever in the rearview
I can't help but briefly think of you
And what could have been
If maybe we first met when
We had more years beneath our belts
I couldn't have imagined that
From all of the ghosts I've encountered
Yours would linger the longest
And I'm sure you don't visit me
When my astral form seeks yours
Still waiting for that coffee date
And starlit drive to sad music

John Queor

Recede

My feelings sink into the Earth
Roots that stretch for miles
Veins that need not be exposed
Kissed by cruelty and weaponry
My walls eclipse the sun
Great and vast like the horizon
Great and vast like the ocean
Calm like sweetened chamomile
Aggressive like a tsunami
Memories buried like bulbs
To one day bloom into a garden
Of varying shades and intensities
Where I will sit in the soft glow
Of the sunlight returned
Flipping through the photo album
Steeping fresh mint tea
Content with the journey
Letting go of the destination

Chasing Sunset

I think one day I'll get out of here
When the universe cracks a path
For me to follow like a map
I'm extremely free but I need more
There's this discomfort that crawls
Beneath my skin when I think of time
The paradox that we are enslaved by
I think I'm getting bored of comfort
I craved this simplicity for so long
And suddenly the grass is dull
This manicured lawn I longed for
Has turned to dreams of pavement
And hastily chasing the sunset
There are so many people out there
With beautiful lives and stories
Now that I'm dry I feel so dull
I could blink and be seventy-eight
It could all end at fifty-five
I really enjoy my life
But I want to feel alive

John Queor

Maine

Liquify myself and return
To the ebb and the flow
Soft lit pastel glow of
Sun slowly climbing
Illuminating the waves
Touching the shore
And opalescent shells
Just scattered
To be gathered
By early travelers
Walking
Wandering
Collecting pieces of
The sea to bring home
And connect with
When she is too far
To be listened to
Or waded in
Or gawked at in wonder
From a seafood shack
On a long pier
Feasting on her children
Twin lobsters
Two sides
$16.95

Oswegatchie River

Once in a while I travel years back
To the grand simplicity of solitude
In a town much smaller than my home
That I did reside in for a short time
And I sometimes get homesick for
Especially on nights I need to breathe
And listen to the rushing river during
The midnight walks from work thinking of
How long until I would escape that place
And find my niche back in the city
Without her ghost surrounding me
Suffocating on a slew of questions
That would arise but never be answered
What a wild decade it's been
I can blink and find myself back
In the passenger seat gazing out
Looking across the pond to Canada
Dreaming about the ghosts in Potsdam
And the love that could have been
But fizzled out like an exhausted flair
A pattern would form from that
A pattern would continue long after

Wild Child

I received a late night phone call
From Panama by my North Star
She's busy bringing gold back
And dancing with the elements
A nomad with a high rise home
And I travel in her pockets

Our exchanges are not frequent
As such with our quick embraces
But it's enough just to know
That although she's ever flowing
When she's home for even an hour
It feels as though no time has elapsed

When she goes I go too
And she wades with me
She is a raging river
I am a calm sea

John Queor

Saintsville

What a long road we had walked
In endless snow that kept falling
Burying us alive in that gazebo
Which was our home for a few hours
Shivering together in cell phone glow
Alive thanks to that structure
And the outlet it offered us
In shock over the altercation
And death of the fruit basket
But you knew a place
Straight down Saintsville
One left and then one right
And then we found warmth
I bought my dog on Saintsville
He's definitely my parents' child
So actually
I bought my brother on Saintsville
Every time I drive down it
I smile and I think of you
And how different things are now
How far we've both come
From our winter hike in that darkness

Two In One

I always thought love would save me
Creep in through all my weathered cracks
Become the great equalizer I had craved
Proving all this fighting was worth something
Skip gleefully towards a marvelous sunset
All while being marveled at and returning it
Yin and yang waltzing towards an end
Being completely okay with it all ending
Because the space between was perfect
And I guess you could say there's still time
And I guess I wouldn't disagree with you
But my appetite for it has dissipated
Like cotton candy caught in a rainstorm
I always thought love would save me
That there would be a moment of clarity
Where I knew everything was everything
I've fallen back to the blue skies before that
Where I could look and see for myself
That an entire world is out there waiting
And I don't necessarily have to be a pair
To find the treasures set out in plain sight
I am two in one and I can be in love
And be the one to save myself

Cutting The Chord

I packed my bags
Then I burnt them
Danced in the smoke
Cried in the sunlight
Felt you leave me
Not to return in spring
Not to haunt me in fall
Banished elsewhere
Reborn somewhere new
And perhaps one day
My soul will find yours
And the stars will align
And the stars will fall
And we'll pack our bags
And we'll burn them
Crying in sunlight

Main Street

I can still hear your voice
In the fog of my memory
Like the blushing horizon
Between sky and sea
Where you speak to me
Despite being someone else
Somewhere else far away
Light-years from this galaxy
I visit our time together
A little less frequently lately
You can not heal a wound
By reopening it repeatedly
But when you come into view
You are welcomed fondly
Along with all the lessons
You graciously shared
With warmth and laughter
I keep them here with me
Beside the crystal ashtray
You placed on the porch
And I thank you dearly
For trusting and listening
To a strange lost boy
In the time elapsed since
The last time I had
Spoken aloud to you
I think I've found myself
And I think you'd be proud

New Paradise

How much more paradise will there be
Those screenshots of absolute peace
I trust-fall into when the light is bleak
Memories too rich to put into speech
I'm not too far gone to continue to
Put out my buckets to continue to
Be filled with childish shrieks of
Laughter and wonder and love
My paradise has not fallen
It's resting on warm grass
Waiting for the bloom
Of moon flowers to
Twist into a crown
To be worn in
A brand new
Paradise

John Queor

It Has All Been Golden

My inner dialogue tells me
This is just the calm before
The storm comes howling
It can't stay gold forever
Has it ever been golden
Am I just perched upon
A line of muted rust
Tricking myself to believe
This has all been priceless
And I get so anxious
Worked up over nothing
Because I know
At the end of the day
Even while panicking
Peace is moments away
And it has been golden

Hourglass

Feeling simultaneously
Too early and too late
Sat in an uncomfortable center
With skin young yet sketching
Plucking a wild gray strand
From the lush amber cascading
Caught in deep pulsing thoughts
As to if I'm closer to the start
Than to the finish line hiding
Crouching out in the open
Just waiting to snatch
Another berry from the vine
Completely stressed out by time
But relaxed comes the morning
To watch a few more lines
Climb this timeless expanse
To ponder this all again
In an endless cycle
Like the infinity sign

Broken Yolk

Do I have a golden center
Or has it gone dull
I'm trying to stay kind
Fighting this persistent
Murky oceanic crashing
Gray blue grasping

Be weary the undertow

Do I protect the child
That resides in my center
Or has he gone pale cold
Lips and eyes the same
Murky oceanic shade of
Glaciers at sunset

Be weary the cold

Do I ever find relief
Or is this what it's like
To never really know
What's still left inside
A list of ghost goodbyes
A possible broken yolk

Route 11

Sometimes I feel as though I've lost too much
And upon a certain angle that statement is true
Mostly when I fixate on what's in the rearview
Shrinking to petite squares that disappear
Monuments that solidified into grand shrines
A two-story home that I once roamed
Where candles twinkled like eyes and stars
Your voice an echo of peace and of power
Reminding me that I can not stay too long
So I move my gaze back to the windshield
With tears forming and a tightened grip
While I visualize what is around the bend
And the people who still occupy my vehicle
Chanting strong spells of encouragement
I find my center in the dance of chaos
The wind whips around me in spirals
I find myself surprisingly unscathed
I find myself drinking in the sunlight
Photosynthesis of my chrysalis
A hybrid of the earth and air
To grow and fly untethered

All The Way In This Time

Without the saturated storm clouds
One couldn't appreciate the sunlight
Falling down on ghost-white skin that
Is undergoing a process of alchemy
I can't remember the very last time
My inside and out were truly golden
I've been pyrite covered in shimmer
Sometimes painting on a smile
Dancing with old skeletons that
Forgave me a very long time ago
And I think I'm ready to let it go now
Let the summer storms cleanse me
Be reborn as the sun climbs
Let peace all the way in this time

John Queor

Sure, I Can Get A Little Bitter

Every time things go up in flames
I get to know myself a little better
Sure, I can get a little bitter
But everything can't be sweet
To sit in my mouth and eat my teeth
Whilst I fall back to reminisce
On moments I could recreate
Nothing has ever been a mistake
Even when I'm up to my chin
In ancient regret and sweet sin
When this is all over
I'll just be back to begin
To get to know myself a little better
And acclimate to the bitterness
So I can truly appreciate the sweet

Reincarnation

Icy tufts of blue whispers
Climbing through the window
Cracked and endlessly inviting
Awaiting an inevitable confabulation
We have had previous altercations
None ending particularly promising
For me no longer breathing

Back to sit betwixt the stars
Awaiting another birthing light
Where I'll become something small
Something bewildered
Something crying
Chasing starlit evenings
Trying to find home

Beacon

I yearn so terribly to
Escape the shore
Where I've sat for years
With foamed tides crashing
Against moss-kissed boulders
As ships sail so delicately
Far off in the distance
Barely aware of my shine
Ushering them closer
So that I may gaze
And admire longingly
Their fantastic travels
Their scuffs and scars
Wishing to see
All that they've seen
On this vast sea
Where I sit quietly
Caressed by her rage
Lulled by her serenity
Tickled by her breeze
But never in her center
Never in her depths
Never anything but
A silly old lighthouse
Who wishes to be free

Water Of The Womb

I've watched cliffs crumble into the sea
Felt them crash into unsuspecting waters
Swallowed to explore her great depths
Sunlight reduced to small sparkles
Kissing the waves
The bubbles
The ripples

My Earth has been corroding
Small pieces have been breaking
Slipping from my closed fist
Like the steady stream of sand
Falling in an hourglass

I will one day crumble into the sea
To fall into the vastness
The darkness
The endlessness
Of time and space
To find myself baptized again
By the sacred water of the womb

Brian

Sometimes it's hard to feel the sun
There's a warmness that is welling
It rises up to the waterline and flows
Sitting on the apple of my cheek
Gazing out and over the city
Before slipping from my chin
To cascade to the cold dry floor
Another summer is among us
It's strange to know that you aren't
There's a long list of names
I never thought would be
Sedimentary memories
Ghost smiles in my dreams

Apollo Alone

Red dot adjacent the center star
Accelerating towards my hands
Outreached as if expecting rainfall
To be decorated in charred debris
As consciousness ascends somewhere

Cradled in slumbers warm embrace
Blowing kisses unto my face
Visions of a dim lit peaceful place
Where I did once forget my grace
But took it back with a hasty pace

In time to witness obliteration
As that dot did decimate
Crashing into the blue and green
Orbiting rock around the center star
Now finding himself much more lonesome

Free Fall

I can't feel your gravity anymore
I used to feel like I was falling
Now I'm stagnant in mid air
Gazing down at what was my home
And lacking interest to even return
I want to find an abandoned shuttle
Drift off to a galaxy I've yet to know
I'm sure my happiness lives there
It was a prophecy that I would land
Right in the palm of your hand
And by some miracle I would stand
And not float off into the cold dark

Diana

Completely fixated on the stillness
Her radiance crawling down
Slipping like silver tears of joy
To fall delicately into my eyes
As I breathe in the moving wind
To let it leave me transformed
Saturated in my deepest dreams
To whoosh and whirl around
To grow likes plants and trees
To kiss the sky and skim the sea
And in time return to me
When the moment is perfect
And my temple is caressed
By her radiance crawling down

John Queor

And Then I Fall Again

Duality
It lacks simplicity
The pillars I dream
To lie between
Surrounded by
Purple nightshade
And ivy vines
Relaxed upon
A satin sheet
I watch the sky
The moon
Her lover
Illuminating me
At the same time
Ménage à trois
Though I am alone
I'm never really alone
Though I am home
I'm not really home
Just relaxing
In this in-between
Until I fall and land
And then I stand
And then I fall again

Find Your Center

The sunlight had been obscured
By a cloud I had summoned once
To blanket me from angelic eyes
Peaking through the sea of stars
To whisper overwhelming secrets
I couldn't decipher at that time
So I conjured a place to hide

Our darkness dwells deep inside
Twisting and clashing with our light
And we believe that one has to win
That one is more just than the other
That our entire lives we must fight
To be a part of the side that is right
Constantly ushered from the center

The whispers I had hidden from
Were just soft summer breezes
Awakening a secret that lived within
Scratching like a cat at the door
Everything works in perfect harmony
All you have to do is take a breath
Release your wars and find your center

Terrence

How magnificent
To have this light
To share
To give away
To receive
Be grateful for
In kind moments
A kettle whistling
Two cups steaming
Rising and
Joining forces
To find healing
To iterate
Our languages of love
Further solidifying
A bond
Pouring laughter
Perspectives
It isn't just blood
That makes
Family

Toss Down Your Silver Strands

Toss down your silver strands
I want to be connected again
To the milky warm blackness
Of the absolute nothingness
That lies in timeless pastures
Caressed by her lullabies

Where I can glance into the mirror
To see who I am and who I will be
As these lessons latch onto me
Like quicksand grains that pull down
But for some reason don't feed
As I slip into the down beneath

Toss down your silver strands
I want to charge my batteries
Taste the static of star shards
The bitterness of reality can be
Washed down with her nectar
Produced by the Milky Way

Present

After discovering the time had come
To gracefully bow out from the poisoning
Another decision followed immediately
That I not set up camp anymore in the past
And that staying present was healthy
But every now and then I glance back for
Only short moments as to not be enticed
To pack a bag and voyage downward
Where I'll be met by a sad reflection
And resort to where I had left off
When I last allowed myself to descend
And slosh around in memories puddles
But better compared to a cold lagoon
I think I'll stay right here on this path
Where for moments I'm sunkissed
Illuminated by what is to come
And not darkened by what already has

Meditation

I sit within
A circle of
Twinkling
Tea lights
To meditate
Transporting
Myself away
From this
Mundane
Monotony
I focus
And transform
This stagnant
Pond into
A static river
And travel
Without
Having to
Leave

And I Will Twist The Knob

Who am I to dream
But dream I do
I slip out from the window
Coast above the city lights
Look for the trap door
To creep into when
The angels aren't looking
In hopes of finding
Crumbs to lead me to
Any sort of clue
As to why
And what
The purpose is
I am grateful
But my curiosity grows
What is the point here
I guess with some patience
The key will be revealed
And I will twist the knob

The As Is

I picked up the fork in the road
And had a slice of decadent cake
It would be a burden to be too beautiful
Completely suffocating I am sure
Probably comparable to choking
On too big a bite of that cake

Forever caught in a coin toss duality of
Being enough and wanting to be more
Often juggling with thoughts of being less
Perhaps even content with the as is
But who is ever really absolutely content
Especially when it boils down to the as is

I set the fork back down in the road
And venture onward more aware
Less focused on coins and cake
Suffocation and a need to change
Deciding that for now the as is
Is completely acceptable

Venue

He opened his arms wide
Gesturing to his surroundings
All of the groupies
And the audiophiles swaying
Screaming, laughing
Singing word for word
He leaned into my ear and said
"This is my church"
I was worshipping with him
In the light show flashing
Hands reached towards heaven
But we were already there
Surrounded by grace
Passing plumes of marijuana
Clouds buzzing in the distance
Preparing to baptize us
His blood in the clouds
His body corn kernels popped
Tossed in salt and sugar

John Queor

Phantom

You spoke to me in a dream last night
Through symbols and varying shades
Hands raised to shield your eyes
Was your mouth a grimace or a smile
Were you peering to see the progress
To assess how much longer to hide
In dark shadows not yet revealed to me
There were moments I didn't feel alone
Though it was only myself occupying
The rectangle in the center of my room
It will remain this way until the spring
When Persephone ascends gracefully
To witness the bulbs burst open
To witness the cold go back to bed
To release you from the darkness
To find yourself within my glow
To whisper the lengths you've gone
To lay hyacinths amongst my duvet

Timeline

There are stars in my eyes
Gazing out there
Nothing in particular
Burdening my dialogue
The inner child
Relaxes reminiscent
Of springs spent
On grass
In trees
Dream inception
Crescent moon
Smoke billowing
Wayward breeze
Innocent laughter
Leaping forward
Falling back
Letting go
Rising
Centered moon
Highest point
And here I am
Gazing out there

John Queor

Retrograde

Venus has abandoned me
Leaving me dry and high
In clouds of contemplation
Collecting drops of dew
Writing poetry under the moon
Sipping grapefruit sparkles
Taking in the breeze
Sharing the wealth
All that now eludes me

Venus has abandoned me
To assist others on their hunt
To be pierced by cupid's arrow
Wearing heart-shaped glasses
And draped in light pink hues
Rubbing honey on their lips
And ylang ylang on their brooms

Venus has abandoned me
I must spend this time alone
To gaze deeply in black mirrors
Until I can clearly see Athena

There's still a war inside
I think I'd like her by my side
When I march at dawn

Almost Viscous

There's this denseness in the air
Almost viscous if you will
Like an uncomfortable caress
Steam fills the lavatory
Lava trickles down my back
How many more until I'm clean
My conscious and my vessel

There's this panic in my skin
Like rotten food in cellophane
Ignored in the vegetable crisper
To ooze out in increments
And I'll find myself fixated on
The fluorescent lighting
Words said in passing
All of my patterns
My addiction to discarding
Wondering why I've kept myself
In such states of discomfort
Without drawing bolder lines

Aware

All of these complexities
Have me ready to pack up
My necessities in a nap sack
And go back to before
The air got so heavy
But I can't remember
A single moment
That I wasn't aware
Of the density of air
And what could be
And what would be lost
In one single blink
Or thirteen years
I'm tired of greetings
I'm sick of goodbyes
And I'm just here vibing
While time is on my side

John Queor

Heavy Air

It's a kind of tired sleep doesn't solve
A burning in the center behind the eyes
Wondering what it would be like
To not feel everything so severely
But teetering on a very frigid numbness
Like a wrong dose of soul Novocaine
I can feel the scraping and prodding
But I can't blink or make a sound
There are times I wonder if I've ever been free
I've always held hands with anxiety
My uncomfortable comfort blanket
Sitting on my chest telling me to breathe
But at this point who would I be without it
It's like a service animal who hurts me
But warns me of the changing pressure
I'm not sure if you've ever felt heavy air
But it's a kind of tired sleep doesn't solve

Lux

I don't want to be a lighthouse anymore
Attracting damaged travelers to my shore
Tending to a kettle and mending bone
Lending an ear to sad voyagers alone
Continuously cleansing with salt and ash
Awaiting another soul to crawl and crash

I want to destroy all the light inside
Put up a closed sign and quietly hide
Extinguish my demons alone with ease
Savor the cool fresh ocean breeze

I don't want to be a lighthouse anymore
But I will never quit and lock my door
For light never truly chooses to elude
Though endless seas taunt to conclude
So I will be the lost souls' ampersand
As a bastion of peace and outstretched hand

Like A Breeze

You're out there
Healing as I am
In preparation to
Find your forever
Butterfly fields
Pastel sunset
A deep longing
To belong
In tender arms
That wrap
And release
And repeat
You're out there
Having conversations
With the same stars
I'm writing letters to

Let's just let love in
Open your window
Let me climb in

Rectangle

There's a calmness found here
In this moment spent alone
In this rectangle I call home
With two candles feasting on
The air that smells of lavender
Smoky notes of Palo Santo
I burnt earlier for a friend
My eyelids are gaining weight
Waiting to be told it's okay
To crash and drift elsewhere
Preferably a summer meadow
Decorated in fragrant flowers
With a brook haphazardly babbling
Giving away her secrets for free
While I wait for one of my angels
To validate the peace I feel
To validate the soft calmness
To shake me gently to wake
To breathe in the *Burnt Lavender* air
In this rectangle I call home
On my rectangle alone
Smothered in serenity

Bloom

He said he'd seen me around a few times
Each time I had been different from the last
He said I was like the bud of a flower
He said he couldn't wait to see me bloom
Which is something we had in common
Which is something I rarely think about
Sometimes I forget that I'm not done
Everything could be just beginning
I feel like I've been so cruel to myself
Sitting in a vase on other people's tables
Always under a certain scrutiny
Mostly under the weight of my own
This body is starting to feel like home
I've occupied the cosmos for so long
Waiting to burst into a billion stars
I think I'll come back down to Earth
Kiss the sun on the mouth
As I make my return
To submerge my roots
Deep in the soil

Imperfect

The hardest part of transformation
Is sitting in the waiting room
Of your own life anticipating how
And when you will be revealed
Days gazing into the mirror
Wondering if it's all worth it
Will there be a moment when
I'm fully satisfied with myself
Will I always have to pretend
And in the midst of my crisis
I look back and see
A person who is no longer me
I'm closer than I've ever been
There's a light inside of me
That once had grown so dim
I'm burning and melting
Dripping into a brand new mold
I am an alchemist
A mad scientist
A work of art
A single cell
A universe
Imperfect

New Electricity

There were times I felt electric
The blue buzz of zesting life
Intoxicated on the spice
The glowing veil of deep night
Turning into neon orange
Pink wisps of laughter
The breeze of a new morning
Conversations while birds sang
Scribbled poetry bathed in
The ash of another cigarette
The splash of vodka soda
The denial of sickness
The not so secret sadness
The neon orange darkened
To aggressive cumulonimbus
I was drowning in the downpour
Inspired by the fast flashes
The full bellied screams of
A sky wanting change
And now I need to find
A new kind of electricity

Of Hyacinths

Imagine if I escaped this sort of stagnant
Tedium that promises to loom over me
If ever I decide to slip into deep comfort
And allow my shoulders to fall slightly
Mimicking the pliability of playdough
Just to discover I detest the new scenery
That I was better off keeping myself behind
Will I smell the adhesive begin to melt
While ascending furiously towards the sun
Could I occupy the orb in liquid form
Or should I stay planted right here
With my wings stuck a decade behind me
And my heart drifting ten years ahead
Where I visualize you waiting for me
To figure out what it is that I want
So the universe can finally provide
And my midnight garden can grow wild
With flowers to decorate ourselves in

Soft Shoe

Soft shoe to the past
Those demons could dance
Amongst other talents
Swimming as an example
Elaborate evenings
Now weighed down in
The dust and soot
Of the days passing
Youth is enticed by speed
Then plagued with longing
As if pace is logical
When you crave everything
This period is for rebuilding
Toning down the ego
And seeing the forest
For the trees
Soft shoe in the dining room
The present is enticing
Hammer in hand
Ready to build
And appreciate the ruins

Winter On James

Frost crystals dance downward
Upon a city mostly sleeping
Yet some are watching
And some are stewing

Unfathomable to ponder
A life with a quiet mind
That can watch and not wonder
Or hurt and not linger

Frost crystals dance downward
Graceful and seemingly peaceful
Perhaps longing to be mimicked
Just allowing life to flow

New Bones

The world is spinning faster than
My mind skydiving without a parachute
Into complex thoughts of situations when
I've needed but couldn't receive
It doesn't quite matter right now though
The Earth is on fire and we may drown
The ice caps that center me are
Dissolving into bacterial sun tea
Perhaps the stars I cling to will
Jump down here to join me
Or whisk me away to a new home
Where things don't feel as serious
Turn me into a gorgeous pastel cloud
Floating and shedding happy tears
Until I've spent all my moisture
I'll sleep for one thousand years
Come back into nice new bones
To a much less parasitic world
Somehow still spinning and thriving
Overgrown with lush greenery
Overtaking the industrial scenery
That took way more than it gave
But deep down to my old bones
I'll wonder how long until it repeats

Icarus

You replaced the sun many years ago
An ideal apparition of you floating
My central perfection to dance around
A love that one could only dream about
Now I can only see you when I dream

The claws of fate play the harp beautifully
Leaving me often in shambles and unruly
To fantasies over adoration so wasted
The candles in my shrine now dust
The mechanics inside of me all rust

You brush the hair from her eyes
And lines grow and I go gray
This wound doesn't seem to heal
No matter how many times I've spun
Around you with your arms crossed

Different Skin

Eons since I've tasted the salty
Crashing roars of water indifferent
Never deciding on a single shade
To dwell on or depth to try and remain
Leaving gifts where it finds its divide
Conscious of healthy boundaries
Until rage shakes her to the core
And suddenly blooms a storm
I'll find you way down in the blue
Blowing bubbles and turning gray
And I'd hate for it to end this way
But to be honest this never ends
It just continues on in different skin

God,

We could meet
In between sky and sea
In the blushing tones
Of pink and sherbet orange
In the fleeting moments
Of the sun descending
And the moon climbing
To sit centered
Receiving cheek kisses
From the star drifting
Into calm slumber
Listening to the ocean
And Sirens singing

We could meet
In the soft static
Of radio waves
Carrying sound to
An old boombox
Sitting outside
Singing to someone
Sunbathing alone
Not even noticing
Our presence
To discuss
What is next

We could meet
At the gate of pearls
Or the river Styx or

Summeland shining
Or before the birth canal
Before the blinding light
A white dove
To perch beside me
And let me know
If I finally graduated
And what it all meant

Deep End

I fall to the moon
As darkness grows
Holding tightly
The slice of peace
I've made my own
Eyes slowly closing
My mind escapes
To venture backwards
To once more reminisce
When I was sunkissed
And calmly floating
In a cool blue pool
Barely worried at all
Unphased by changes
Unknowingly creeping
As I lie basking
Relaxed and aloof

Fruit Of The Forest

All of the loss has lead me here
My eyes and heart are wide open
Letting the scent of wildflowers flow
In through each of the windows ajar
In exchange for this beautiful outlook
I'll set out a fruit of the forest pie
To waft in the direction of those lost
Guiding them to my welcome mat
Come sit with me at the table
I'll prepare us a pot of tea
Tell me your entire story
Even the details you keep below
In the dusted basement growing mold
We may enter and leave this world alone
But while you trot on this soil
You are not alone

Ghastly Gust

These nightmares could evaporate into
Silver lining moonbeam bouquets
Blooming when the sky is darkest
Like the ghosts of aromatic gardenias
Plucked and waiting for the wind
Where they will forcibly frolic askew

I could try once more to rest my eyes
And face the wall of water waiting
To crash upon me and drag me out
To an ever-changing dirtless grave

These nightmares could transform into
Da Vinci Code-style maps to guide me
Through figuring out the roots grounded
Fueling the fear interrupting pastel resting
I don't want to be a gardenia plucked
In a hurry waiting for that ghastly gust

Haunted House

There are a couple boxes left in the attic
They're probably not that important
But I can't shake the need to go check
Turning the corners of bare rooms
Where once sprawled out my roots
Echoes of laughter and crying
Residual warmth of dancing candles
Scuffs from furniture and broken glass
Walls that will soon be painted white
Eavesdropping on new conversations
I slink up the creaking stairway
Dust particles meandering in sunlight
Gifted by a bare window greeting me
Before I turn the knob to the attic
Before I'm welcomed by the smell of old
Cobwebs slightly swaying from the drafts
Two boxes sit beneath a sun window
I sit criss-crossed and begin to rummage
Through the bigger box on my left
I find an album of old photographs
From what I gather I just never left

Conspiracy Board

I'm writing this as a farewell
I'm letting the ghosts find the light
I've held so tightly to my pain
My uncomfortable security blanket
Flashbacks to the darkest times
Stealing space for more stars
To cluster closer together
Creating a tunnel to step into
I'll have all of the answers
Surrounded in absolute white
God will gaze at my conspiracy board
And make the correct connections
I'll gasp when I step back
Validated that everything
Had happened for a reason
And I'll move on to what's next

John Queor

Karat

Go on and fix yourself
Drape yourself in gold foil
Slow spin like a glass ball
It's all reflection anyway

You'll soon realize
Your demons are asleep
But you're still awake
And nothing feels different

Go on and fix yourself
Collect all those thoughts
It's all so haphazard
It's all reflection anyway

Midnight Is Never Elusive

Midnight is never elusive
Even in the sun at noon
I can pace in blue dark
Surrounded by the stars
Sipping my nostalgia
Like bitter root tea
But as the years grow
The brew gets sweet

The past used to terrify me
I'd dilute the goblet with ice
Dive into my discomfort
Sleep there for the night

Midnight is never elusive
It's just one breath away
My eyes close and I'm home
But also so far away
And I can see so clearly
That there was a point
And there is a destination
And I don't have to stay

Caught in the moment

John Queor

This Is The Process

I've had love
Discard it
Circled the drain thrice
Don't touch me please
I'm in the process

Humanoid carbon copy
If you thirst for me
I'll watch you drown
Bubbles always fascinated

I've had love
Hoard it
Circle on my brow bone
Touch me, need me
This is the process

Star Fire

And there's hope
Two flames that bend
Ready to reach
Hoping to not be burned

Turbulence is anticipated
Your touch is craved
If there's pain
At least there was hope

Wrap this vessel in love
And wait to be reciprocated
This soul is star fire
And it has much to give

Bloodlet

Mend these broken bones with gold
The small cracks that I'm ignoring
I'm having an out of body experience
Sometimes I wish I could just discard it
Find paradise inside a quaint black hole
A comfortable cottage up in the stars
But my work here is just beginning
And these inconveniences are blips
Of an incredible montage I'm making
I'll be doing collages with Sarah soon
I'll bloodlet my art on construction paper
Black and white cut up photographs
All of this reminiscing is inspirational
I'll tell you the rest when I'm older

Like A Splitting Atom

I think about you
But I don't want to think about you
I don't want to think about myself
I want a quiet corner to recline in
Listening to the static of nothing
Void of my false optimism
Void of my pessimistic whispers
I need a few moments in the blue black
Like the oily pigment of a raven's back
That I could request to climb upon
And abandon myself for a while
Or I could just descend
Sink into the mattress
Through the floor
Beneath the concrete
Into the compact dirt
Until I find the core
I feel too much lately
I need to ground
I need to find the center
I need to explode
Like a splitting atom

Chill

Condensation makes me wish
I too could transfer to
The other side of the glass
I've been spending such copious
Amounts of time looking within
Answers alluding and going dim
I'll find Nirvana sometime later
When I've clawed to the surface
In time for an ocean wave to crash
And by some chance I won't drown
But ponder the odds forever
Knowing everything will crumble
Just as soon as I get comfortable
Exhaling and leaning back into
The plastic-wrapped recliner
As the universe turns to ash
But not before I release a laugh
Because I knew it was coming
And I knew that I was going

Refuse To Fuse

There are things I think I want
But hastily dissuade myself
When I see the bigger picture
Unfolding itself as I gaze up
To the white textured ceiling

There is immense pressure
To cross things off the list
Like a visit to the supermarket
With only a minute time limit
And I'm distracted easily

There are moments of clarity
Where I feel like I'm on track
And days that I feel like a feather
Caught in an angry gust
Waiting to fall back onto solid ground

There is a war inside of me
A duality of peace and terror
Both sides are necessary
Both sides speak the truth
Both sides refuse to fuse

Until now

Soda

The tantalizing bubbles rising
Flute pressed to my lips
To drain the liquid and
Temporarily leave myself
Until afternoon brought me back

Sometimes that void is mourned
But to rise with sun rays
Makes this progress worth while
Worth continuing this dry spell
And facing my demons soundly

Bass vibrates through the window
A party is being thrown down the street
And I've just had my second club soda
In an oversized wine glass
Reminiscing on my twenties

NO
STOPPING
ANY
TIME

NOV 1 - APR 1
OVERNIGHT
PERMITS
FROM
10 PM 300 DAYS

6 AM EVEN DAYS

Rearrange

All the times I thought I had lost myself
Were just chaotic flashes of change
I rearranged the scenery a few times
I felt loss every single time
There is no growth in one fish bowl
I learn something new everywhere
I meditate and go back to other homes
Inhale the soft sparkles and hard nails
The welcomes and goodbyes spinning
Much like a rotary door
You never know the last time
You'll feel at home at a home
You once sprawled out in
Breaking bread and laughing
Sleeping soundly and safe
But you can't grow in one fish bowl
All the times I thought I had lost myself
Were moments I became more free
I just had to rearrange the scenery

Venus Is Crying

Venture to our secret place
Even in storms severe
No one can keep me away
Under your galaxy shrine
Simmer in my longing

Incredible how long I've held onto
Something so awfully pointless

Certainly I will be released
Rid myself of this obsession
Your image to one day fade
Ice melting to evaporate
Noticing a weight lifting
Glimpses of finding freedom

Falling

When I begin to feel it unravel
I lie back and allow it
What good does it do
To stay wound up so tightly

Within this soft skin cell
Lives the energy of a star
Pulsing and waiting
To tear it's way out
And find its way home
To reflect on this experience

Burn alone in rage
Twinkle in sweet bliss
Fall back to the earth
Starved for your love
To search for your soul
Sunbathe in your scar garden

Rest and repeat

Lovely Labyrinth

It is easy to lose way in this labyrinth
But even in moments that I felt lost
I always learned something new
And expressed my full gratitude
For aiding me in my transformation
For which there will be no end
Because everything transfers
From rivers into oceans to
Evaporating up to great clouds
That hold for just a little while
But in decades or seconds release
And we all descend again
To get lost in this lovely labyrinth
Until we graduate to one greater
In the presence of a different sun
New strange constellations to
Base our personalities on

Neat

What if the poison was sweet
Labeled safe for consumption
But only in miniscule increments
Sometimes I miss the potions
That allowed my brain a break
But stole ten years away
Blurring nights and weekends
Anxiety filled mornings
Where I wouldn't turn on my phone
Because I knew I did something wrong

Even though I know I'm better off
Keeping the nectar from my lips
I can hear its soft whispers
To return for just a while
Quickly blacken out the day
But I know if I go back once
I will absolutely stay
The games I thought I loved
I no longer want to play

Dream Seed

My dreams are quite simple
Half of them are with me
My thoughts swarm free
Sky full of dandelion seeds
And when the wind is tired
They'll find their homes
Set down their little roots
Snack on the rain and sun
And when I forget them
That's when they'll bloom
I'll see their children
Carried back to me
In a cool gentle gust
I'll whisper them stories
Of the beauty of their mothers
And how they gave so much to me

Sink

Cast my gaze into smooth obsidian
Let myself find what sleeps inside
What creeps around my subconscious
The entities that dance during daylight
Warmth that only August can provide
Releasing me from the murky seas
Where I've added my own dashes of salt
To be my sacrifice and second as an offering
I can hear the lions roar around me
Rolling in the sand and sweet grass
I will only take that which I need
Submerged in the darkest depths
Imagery flashing all around me
Endlessness ahead and behind
And I sink but I'm centered
And I sink but I'm home
And I sink but I'm free

The Good Blue

Yesterday I was sloshing around
In a pyrex coffin filled to the brim
With American vodka and cigarette swirls
Waiting hastily to be returned to the Earth
Waiting for the burnt morning sun beams
To kiss my forehead and tuck me into bed
To wake late afternoon filled up with dread
Nauseous with a headache from the poisoning
That always disoriented instead of removed me
It felt like I would never come up for air
I was caught in a web of smoke and ash
Bourbon soaked tissues and bed sheets
And I thought that was all there was to be
To fizzle out in my toxic rituals and routines
Tomorrow I will be sloshing around
In the refreshing embrace of a lake
Where I'll lounge grateful and sunkissed
Relaxing beneath the good blue
Where I'll express my thank yous

Swim

I'm ready to be baptized again
In the frigid crashing waters
Of the beautiful pacific
Submerged until absolved
My sins as skin particles
Flaking off to join the sand
My nonverbal confessions
A very relaxed choreography
God watching from the window
And when asked if they liked it
Chortle and say "Sure, kid"

2B2BS

Pressure and time
Will one day sparkle
Circling your finger
You feel the stress
But are ignorant to
What it can do for you

Release a steady exhale
Everything is fine
And even if it's not
What's the worse
That can happen to something
Endless

Fixation

Angels lose their radiance
When a smile sweeps your face
And the devil's blood does boil
Merely thinking of your grace
The cosmos practices gratitude
Knowing you occupy their space
I close my eyes to mediate
Of how wondrous you must taste

It is not only lust which plagues my mind
I'm honored to bask in your aura alone
Get high on being inside of your brain
Baptized by the air leaving your lungs

Angels lose their wings
To walk the earth beside you
And the devil does ascend to
Tempt and get inside you
The cosmos shimmers light
To protect and guide you
I close my eyes to meditate
On how blessed I'll be to find you

Static

I want to be lightning flashes
Sprinting across your sky
To gently catch your eyes
Ascend and briefly hide
To ignite before you again
Before you put yourself to bed
And fight the tired covering you
To quietly pray that I explode
Before you drift to dream of me
Spread on swaying grass blades
Waiting to be caressed by you
And the refreshing breeze
That dishevels your soft strands
And whispers into my eyelashes
Pointed right in your direction
Inviting you to sprawl with me
In the brief moments right before
Evaporating back into the air
And when you try to remember me
There will be flashes everywhere

Fitting In

For a while I was shocked to see eighteen
How do you progress past a point unknown
I could see the world but not where I fit in
There were places for circles and squares
Even triangles had an opening to slip into
There were no slots for an irregular decagon
Sometimes resembling thorns others a star
Sometimes I sent out angry prayers to God
Demanding that he fix all of these mistakes
I've always been different in many ways
I'd hoped that my strangeness was a phase
Dissipating with the awkwardness of youth
Being young is hard in so many ways
Expectations, being seen, dodging the radar
I realized one night that I wasn't broken
And my peculiarities were great parts of me
I apologized for each of those angry prayers
I started to write letters of gratitude
I'm not like a single person I know
Isn't that fantastic

Resembling A Moth

Reflection has been key
Engulfed in perspective
Seeing it all as it is
Especially the dark parts
Marveling at the freedom
Born from release
Lounging in the sun spots
Incredible warmth surrounding
Never to go too far
Gaining control

Annihilating my demons

Moving up and away
Over the elements
To let the light baptize me
Halcyon winds remove the dust

Field Of Weeds

Sun descends in a familiar place
Tree branches sway in purple breeze
Pastel hues melt deep in the horizon
Where the light slips down beneath

Grass stops glowing as stars form
And the forest becomes a silhouette
Birds' songs lull to almost perfect silence
Broken by the cricket symphony

Bass vibrates through bone
Back to where was my home
I've seen this picture many times
But it feels even nicer to dive back in

Life Cycle

Trees release their leaves
Kissed by the colors of death
Ogled at and crunched on
In preparation for the white
To blanket the cold ground
I am shaking myself free
Readying my long limbs
To once again be renewed
Fresh sprouts will cover me
With the exhale of spring
Caterpillars finding home
Feeding from my greenery
To very soon rest on my bark
Wings extended and ready
To be allied with the wind

Equinox

I know
This is all very heavy
It's supposed to be
Pressure is necessary
To destroy the dam
Unclog the drain
Send me down a vortex
I'll meet myself in the middle
Like an equinox
Half of me lying in the sun
Half of me dancing in the moon
All of me functioning as a whole
Full of understanding and gratitude

Divorce

I spent a lot of time with rage
I got to know him very well
For a while I thought it was love
His intensity inspired and scared me
In the very beginning
His thoughts on vengeance
And the acceleration of karma
Spoke to me molecularly
We picked blood-red roses
Holding hands in death's valley
I felt happy with him
But it soon became relentless
There could be no simplicity
Everything was a master plan
Everything was done on purpose
Everything happened to us
Due to perspective we divorced
I detoxed to get the poison out
We cross paths now and again
He sometimes reaches for my hand
But I'm engaged to peace now
We meditate in fields of fruit
We let our tears feed the earth

Rearview

Paradise had fallen behind me
The remains of descending leaves
Gathered in a big pile of which was
Like most great and wonderful things
Dived into and not appreciated enough

I find more joy returning to those times
Than what I actually probably
Felt in those moments
Just a very young boy
Heart fast-beating
Never really thinking
Just leaping

Paradise has fallen behind me
Where I glance every chance
In the rearview mirror while
I drive further away
Watching details disappear
Like unshaking a Polaroid

Autumn In Potsdam

I walked through fallen leaves
Alone with my thoughts at three
Admiring the saturation of dark sky
And how quiet the streets had become
Cigarette smoke swirling and rising
And I wondered if you were exhaling
A plume of carcinogens at the same time
Immersed in the same eerie darkness
Thinking of me and what could be
I like to press my face against
The windows of the past so that
I don't fully reintroduce the poison of
The same old avoidable tragic mishaps
But I also like to remember myself smiling
And how incredible it was to feel
To love with everything I had
The freedom of feeling without knowing
How exhausting it would become
When for a while my butterflies
Transformed into hornets

John Queor

Sound Bath

Even on the worst days
Relief was always a reach away
Melodies to sigh and soothe
Providing a purpose to remain
I surrounded myself in sound
It made me feel understood
Music is my therapist
Often doubling as my muse
Delivering light to the depths
Carrying me back to the surface
Where I'm hugged by the sun
Until my bones are warm again

Closed Casket

I think it's time to rest now
Climb into the pine box
Listen to the kind words
You are completely free
To venture the cosmos
Sleep for a century
Return as a fresh shadow
To haunt someone new
I think I'm ready to begin again
Let my dreams seep into me
Melt into my straight shoulders
Not dipping or leaning any longer
Veins once more full of gold
Pupils examining the road ahead
Keeping peace and releasing dread

John Queor

I love you, Mom and Dad

Hover

The sand shifted beneath me
Embracing me with dry heat
I walked down to the waves
Softly massaging the shore
I breathed with the pattern
I visualized all of my good
I waded peacefully in the water
Until my feet no longer connected
Allowing me to hover
To let go of the connection
To feel free for a moment
Before appreciating the support
Being held like a baby
And in the midst of the baptism
I reflected on my parents
There was a period when
Their love was hard ground
But with time did
Transform into soft sand
Turning into liquid
Then reminding me
They were always there
Even when I didn't feel connected

Saturn Return

Saturn has returned to me
All of my debts are paid
One contribution to the air
Lightening around me now
Soon the slate will be fresh
My land will be leveled
In preparation to build
A beautiful life
With what time I still have
With the lessons I've learned
With the people I love
Saturn might your rings surround me
Might you bless and protect me
There are still battles left
That I'll finish when I visit Mars

Mars

Oftentimes I felt like a hand grenade
A calm meadow quickly turned into a crater
Debris to float down like snow for weeks
The surrounding grass crisp and black
And I wouldn't have been there to see
To experience the damage I created
In the midst of my combustion
Never able to collect myself again
To nurse the land back to health
My battles are billowing sea breezes
They're acknowledged and released
I don't collect them in jars anymore
Like fireflies that steal the light
My reactions are the counterstrikes
Incredibly calm and peaceful
Oftentimes I feel like a hand grenade pin
And I have no plans to be pulled
I have found control

Expanse

Perhaps my reflection is not the best place
To question whether any of this is real
But he reminds me that we are spinning
On a rock moving through endlessness
Created from an explosion that won't stop
And even when it's over it's very likely
To continue on without stopping

I find it horrifying but interesting
In the same vastly strange way
That the world grows and shrinks daily
Expanding and collapsing like a lung
Hoarding oxygen to scream into the void
And quickly landing back on Earth
Peering through the bathroom mirror
Blinking in tremendous shock
As the universe swirls in our irises

10%

There's a billion things going on
Around my aura stationed calmly
Beneath the pitter patter of water
Dancing from my body to the drain
And my mind is filling up with
Static as it tunes into a station
Of memories like fireflies
Shooting caution warnings
Behind my eyelids falling closed
Along with a few voices
Bouncing haphazardly around
And I remind myself it's dangerous
To venture too deep
And that I should try and sleep
Instead of playing with a puzzle
That I know can't be complete

John Queor

Regenerate

Don't be afraid of the process
The nights you kept yourself awake
Tossing and turning and shedding
Fifteen gallons of saltwater
Was only a way of exfoliating
Executing old skin cells
In preparation for a birth

After a few years you will be new
To walk the earth untouched
By the ghosts you thought
Would never let go

CLARITY

Captured by my own mind
Letting walls surround me
Anticipating endings that
Remain deep in hiding
Insisting that I let go of all
That's been keeping me fuzzy
Years add up no matter what

Caught in a moment of distress
Leaping into faith's cupped hands
Awaiting the overflow as I sink in
Ready to breathe in this spring
I thought I'd never get out
That I'd be kept forever
Yearning for clarity

Crystal clear glass stares back
Leaving the air a little lighter
All the dirt circling the drain
Refreshed and filtered
I needed this time to heal
To scrub from the inside out
Years add up no matter what

I Look Around And Smile

I look around and smile
There's happiness here
It's definitely not perfect
But I don't strive for that
I've always wanted simplicity
I've never really known it
But I knew I would know
When I finally found it
And I find myself here
Looking around
Silently remembering
All the chaos
I used to invite in
And it was so fun
Sometimes so sad
I'll cherish the people
I'll cherish the places
I'll let go of the things
That keep me from staying
Golden
I hope you find the gold too
I hope you choose to shine
Be bright
And be kind
Shake off the dust and fly

To Be Is Just To Be

You are but a star shard
Swaying in the dark
A fragment of everything
The size of a cell
One fiber of the seed
Of a dandelion breeze
Drinking in the sunshine
Galavanting in the sea
At the end of the day
To be is just to be

Toodles

Let me slip into something more comfortable
I remove my skin suit and burst into a galaxy
It's easier to show you exactly how I feel
I've tamed my rage and acclimated to
The sadness that makes it hard to rise
But I don't feel those things all of the time
I spend a lot of time appreciating simple things
Nestled under the soft blankets of calmness
Love is tricky for me but I'm familiar with it
Joy and I spend time together every day
I laugh like a maniac when something is funny
I almost always can find something funny
I always try to focus on the brightest side
My light may dim some days but it's always on
I talk to the universe every single night
I express my gratitude and ask for blessings
For all of my family and closest friends
My darkness only makes up half of me
Although for a while I felt like Alaska
But that's a whole other book
I've found a healthy balance for myself
All of these experiences were a blessing
Let me slip into something more comfortable
I exit out the back door without saying bye

Notes on Poems

Medicinal, the line "Listening to *No Quarter*" refers to the song *No Quarter* by Led Zeppelin.

Sunshine Paradise is dedicated to Brian, Ashlee, Drew, Joanna and Josh.

The photograph accompanied by the poem **Tolerance** was taken at the first bar I ever did a poetry reading in.

The photograph accompanied by the poem **Give It To Myself** was taken by Bo, a regular at my bar.

Maine was inspired by a memory of picking seashells with my grandmother in Maine.

It Has All Been Golden, the line "It can't stay gold forever " is a reference to *The Outsiders* by S. E. Hinton. "Stay gold" is a reference to the Robert Frost poem that Ponyboy recites to Johnny where one line reads, "Nothing gold can stay."

The photograph accompanied by the poem **Venue** is of the band The Decemberists.

Icarus is a continuation of the poem **Satyr** in my debut poetry collection, *Burnt Lavender*.

Haunted House is an alternate ending to the poem **Visit** in *Burnt Lavender*. It's what I'd imagine would have happened if I hadn't left the attic when I did.

The photograph accompanied by the poem **Bloodlet** is of Sarah, who I'll be doing collages with. Her Instagram is @kn_own_liar.

Closed Casket is a continuation of the poem **Husk** in *Burnt Lavender*.

The photograph accompanied by the poem **I Look Around And Smile** was taken by Matty K.

189

Acknowledgments

Thank you so much
to all of my family and friends who
believe in and support me.

To my Grandma, thank you for supporting me through all of my
phases and enlightenments. I know I've never been an easy
person to follow, but you have been behind me each step!
Love you, Grandma!

Thank you to Indie Earth Publishing
for helping me turn my dream into reality.

Thank you, reader,
for taking this journey with me.

About the Author

© John Queor

John Queor is a queer poet, scribbling most of his work while cloaked in the early morning darkness. John resides in central New York, but one day hopes to live in Maine, in a small cottage by the sea.

Connect with John on Instagram:
@johnnyqu33r

More Books by John Queor:
Burnt Lavender

Featured Anthologies:
The Spell Jar: Poetry for the Modern Witch
Dreams In Hiding: an almagation of verses & prose

About the Publisher

INDIE EARTH

PUBLISHING

Indie Earth Publishing Inc. is an independent, author-first co-publishing company based in Miami, FL, dedicated to giving writers the creative freedom they deserve when publishing their poetry, fiction, and short story collections. Indie Earth provides its authors a plethora of services meant to aid them in their book publishing experiences and finally feel they are releasing the book of their dreams.

With Indie Earth Publishing, you are more than just an author, you are part of the Indie Earth creative family, making a difference one book at a time.

www.indieearthbooks.com

For inquiries, please email:
indieearthpublishinghouse@gmail.com

Instagram: @indieearthbooks

9 798986 989891